21st **Century Skills** INNOVATION LIBRARY

UNOFFICIAL
GUIDES

ANIMAL CROSSING:
Beginner's Guide

CHERRY LAKE PUBLISHING • ANN ARBOR, MICHIGAN

by Josh Gregory

T0027064

CHERRY LAKE PRESS

Published in the United States of America by Cherry Lake Publishing
Ann Arbor, Michigan
www.cherrylakepublishing.com

Reading Adviser: Beth Walker Gambro, MS, Ed., Reading Consultant, Yorkville, IL
Photo Credits: ©Vantage_DS/Shutterstock, 6

Cherry Lake Press is an imprint of Cherry Lake Publishing Group

Library of Congress Cataloging-in-Publication Data has been filed and is available
at catalog.loc.gov

Cherry Lake Publishing Group would like to acknowledge the work of the Part-
nership for 21st Century Learning, a Network of Battelle for Kids. Please visit
http://www.batelleforkids.org/networks/p21 for more information.

Printed in the United States of America
Corporate Graphics

Contents

Chapter 1

Island Life

Have you ever dreamed about living on an island paradise? Have you ever wanted to decorate your own house or design your own clothes? What about starting your own town with a small group of good friends? What if you could do all of these

That means living each day to the fullest, doing things I like, and having lots of fun!

Animal Crossing is full of positivity and good vibes. Your character doesn't face any threats or deadlines, so you can relax while playing.

Canberra

Hey! I'm trying to be more neighborly and get to know folks better, and I wanna know about you. That cool?

You can get to know hundreds of different animal characters during your *Animal Crossing* adventures.

things without ever leaving your house? Believe it or not, you can. All you need to do is play *Animal Crossing: New Horizons*!

New Horizons, the latest game in the long-running *Animal Crossing* series, became a worldwide sensation when it was released for the Nintendo Switch in early 2020. *Animal Crossing* isn't like other games. Players don't compete with each other or work to defeat enemies. The game isn't fast-paced or focused on action. There is no way to win or lose. Instead, *Animal Crossing* gives players a relaxing environment to be creative, meet up with friends online, and explore a **virtual** world.

Interested in trying *Animal Crossing* for yourself? All you need is a Nintendo Switch and a copy of the game. For certain in-game features to work correctly, you'll also need a wireless internet connection, but it's not required to get started.

When you start up the game for the first time, you'll find yourself in the offices of a business called

You can play *Animal Crossing* on the go or enjoy it on the big screen by docking your Nintendo Switch.

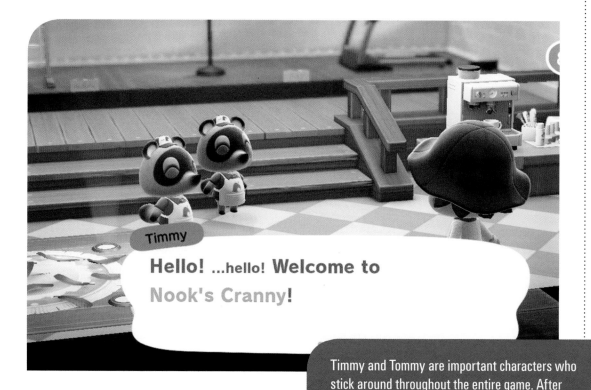

> Timmy
>
> **Hello!** ...hello! **Welcome to Nook's Cranny!**

Timmy and Tommy are important characters who stick around throughout the entire game. After you reach the island they will eventually open a general store.

Nook Inc. There, you will meet Timmy and Tommy Nook, two cute **tanukis** who are offering a "deserted island getaway package." This getaway package is the beginning of your journey into the world of *Animal Crossing*. To start, you'll need to answer a few questions for Timmy and Tommy. First, tell them the name and birthday you want your character to have. Most players use their real birthdays, and you can also use your real first name if you want. (*Animal Crossing* does a good job of keeping your private information safe from strangers if you decide to play online.) However, you can use whatever name and date you like. Just remember that you can't change these things once you start playing.

Next, Timmy and Tommy need to take a picture of your character. This is your first opportunity to change your character's appearance. You can pick between different hairstyles, skin colors, and facial features. Choose whatever you like, and don't worry

Your character represents you in the world of *Animal Crossing,* but it doesn't have to look like you unless you want it to.

Characters in *Animal Crossing* experience the same seasonal weather and holidays as people in real life.

if you can't get it just right. You'll get the chance to change your character's looks as often as you like once you start playing. You'll also unlock all kinds of new styles that aren't available at first.

The next thing you need to do is let Timmy and Tommy know whether you live in the Northern or Southern **hemisphere**. In *Animal Crossing*, time passes and seasons change just like they do in real life. If you play at night, it will be nighttime in the game. If you play during winter, it will be winter in the game. The two hemispheres have their seasons at different times of year. This means you'll need to answer the question honestly if you want the game's seasons to match the ones you experience in real life.

Next up is another important decision. Timmy and Tommy will show you four potential layouts for your island. These are random, so every player will get slightly different options. However, all possible choices have a few things in common, such as a river that runs across the island and beaches along the edges. No matter which layout you choose, you will

Every possible island layout contains plenty of places to go fishing!

Animal Crossing is designed to be played every day, or as close to every day as players can manage, for short bursts of time. The longer players continue to do this, the more they will get to see and experience in the game's ever-changing world. Unless *Animal Crossing* is the only game you play on your Switch, you'll need to close and reopen it frequently. When you are done playing for the day, be sure to save your progress and quit through the in-game menu before you fire up a different game.

If you need to take a break from playing *Animal Crossing*, but you plan on coming back to the game instead of playing something else, you can use the Switch's sleep function. When you are ready to get back to playing, simply wake the system up and you can pick up right where you left off. You won't need to wait for the game to start up and load. This can really be a handy time-saver!

still be able to do all of the same things in the game. And later on, once you've played a while, you'll get the chance to change your island's layout. You'll be stuck with your choice for quite a while, though, so pick a layout that looks good to you!

After you pick an island layout, you can feel free to answer the final question from Timmy and Tommy however you like. Your decision won't change anything in the game. All that's left to do after that is board the plane and head to your new home!

Chapter 2

Settling In

After you land, you'll find yourself at the small airport on the southern coast of your island. Timmy and Tommy will be there, and so will two animal villagers who have joined the deserted island getaway along with your character. After a short scene, everyone will head to the **plaza** area in the center of the island. The plaza is an important area

At first, your island's plaza will look pretty empty.

Later on, Tom Nook's tent will become the Resident Services building.

that you will return to over and over again as you play. For now, you're there to meet a character named Tom Nook. Like Timmy and Tommy, Tom Nook is a tanuki. He is also the owner of Nook Inc., and he will give you goals to work toward throughout *Animal Crossing: New Horizons*.

The first thing Tom asks you to do is find a place on the island to set up your tent. You can pick any location you want, but choose carefully. The location you pick for your tent will soon become the site of a more permanent house. You can eventually move your house's location, but it will take a long time to reach that point. It will also cost you a lot of in-game money to do.

Building up your home and collecting furniture and other objects to decorate the inside is a big part of *Animal Crossing*. You'll also be in charge of building and arranging other structures on the island, with the goal of creating a whole town full of colorful characters. In fact, Tom Nook's next task for you will be

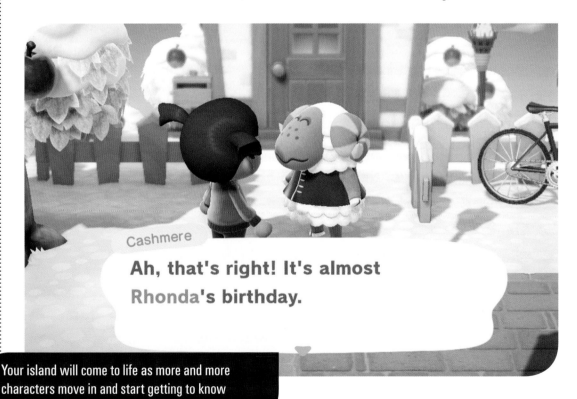

Cashmere

Ah, that's right! It's almost Rhonda's birthday.

Your island will come to life as more and more characters move in and start getting to know one another.

Sea snail

:48 PM

y 20 (Wed.)

Stand near objects on the ground to find out what they are. Then press the Y button to pick them up.

to choose locations for your two neighbors' homes. It works just like choosing the location for your own home. After you're done, Tom will ask you to collect some supplies to throw a welcome party in the plaza. This is a great introduction to one of the main activities in *Animal Crossing*: gathering items from around the island. Follow the instructions to collect some tree branches and fruit. Once you're ready, the celebratory campfire can begin. Tom will ask you to give your island a name. Choose carefully, because you won't be able to change it later.

As the campfire is winding down, Tom Nook will give you a cot and suggest that you go to sleep in

Ring Those Bells

Money in *Animal Crossing* is called Bells. You'll start out with nothing in your wallet, but soon you'll be spending tens of thousands at a time with no worries. It will take a lot of Bells to build up your town, buy the latest fashions, and decorate your home. The best ways to make money early on are to collect fruit, seashells, bugs, and **fossils** around the island and sell them to Timmy and Tommy. Once you have some supplies built up, you can also **craft** items to sell. Before you start crafting, check with Timmy and Tommy to see which items they are paying the most Bells for. It changes every day, so check back frequently.

There is also another type of **currency** called Nook Miles. You earn them by completing special tasks on an app on your NookPhone. You can exchange Nook Miles for special items that often can't be found in regular stores. You can also use them to purchase tickets to visit other islands, or simply exchange them for Bells.

your tent. Take his advice and head inside. You'll find a lantern and a radio packed up in boxes. Unpack them, then open up your **inventory** and get out the cot Tom gave you. Inside your tent, you can arrange these items however you like. You can also turn the lantern and radio on or off if you like. As your home grows and you collect more items, you'll soon have all kinds of options for decorating. Take a minute to get used to the controls for placing, moving, and interacting with objects. Moving the right stick on the controller will let you move the camera around to see the room from different angles. You can also pick up any item and put it in your pocket to return it to your inventory. Once you're done, move your character toward the cot to lie down and go to sleep.

Once you wake up from your nap, Tom Nook will give you a NookPhone and show you how to use it. He'll also let you know that you owe him money to pay

Get to know the different apps on your NookPhone. You'll be using them a lot throughout the game.

for the trip! After that, you'll be free to start playing the game how you like. In *Animal Crossing*, you are free to do what you want at any time. Tom Nook will give you tasks to complete, but there is never a time limit to complete them. You can also take as long as you want to repay the money you owe him. There are no penalties, and you can't mess anything up. Take your time and relax as you play!

One of the main things you should do almost every day is go around the island and collect all of the various supplies you find. Tree branches are an important resource for crafting. Sometimes they will be lying on the ground. You can also shake trees to make more branches fall down. If the tree has fruit, that will fall down too. Pick it up! You can sell fruits or plant them to grow new fruit trees. Near beaches, you'll find a variety of seashells. Pick those up too. They're worth money!

Crafting is one of the most essential skills in *Animal Crossing*. To get started, simply approach a crafting table. You'll find one in the plaza, to start. Later, you can build different crafting tables and place them wherever you like. When you're at the crafting table, you'll see a list of all the DIY (do-it-yourself) recipes you have found so far. Each recipe requires a different set of supplies. As long as you have the right supplies in your inventory, you'll be able to craft that item.

You'll want to focus on getting some tools as soon as you can. Tools will allow you to collect even more resources, and they are required to complete many tasks in the game. For example, you can't go fishing until you have a fishing rod, and you can't dig up fossils without a shovel. You can purchase "flimsy" versions of the tools from Timmy and Tommy. These are the most basic versions of the game's tools, and they will break after just a few uses. If you want to create more **durable** versions, you'll need to get DIY recipes and craft them.

You can unlock an item called the tool ring. It lets you quickly switch between your tools by pressing the up arrow button.

Chapter 3

Building Up

Want to start building up your town and unlocking new features to play with? Talk to Tom Nook. In fact, it's a good idea to chat with Tom anytime you find yourself wondering what to do next. He will always have new tasks to suggest for you. They might involve gathering different materials or helping build a new business on the island. Usually,

Every time a new building is finished, the island's residents will gather to celebrate.

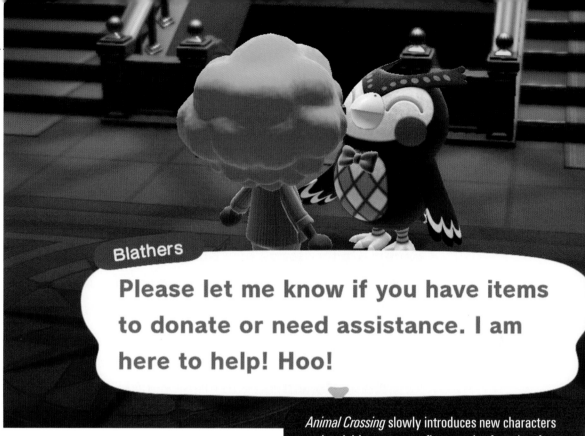

Blathers

Please let me know if you have items to donate or need assistance. I am here to help! Hoo!

Animal Crossing slowly introduces new characters and activities over your first couple of weeks of playing. This gives new players a chance to learn everything without getting overwhelmed.

you will learn about a new feature or get some kind of valuable reward each time you complete one of Tom's requests.

In most games, you can keep making progress by simply playing more. But in *Animal Crossing*, time passes just like in real life. Sometimes you might find yourself running out of things to do for the day. Or it might take a couple of days of waiting before a new building is finished. This is especially true during the first couple of weeks after you start playing. During this time, you will gradually see important features such as shops and a museum appear on your island. New animal villagers will slowly move in. Little by little, you'll see your island start to grow. Just be patient, do the things Tom Nook asks of you, and follow your daily routine of gathering supplies.

Once you have a fishing rod and a net, try to start catching the various fish, bugs, and other wildlife on the island. One you've caught something, bring it to Tom Nook. He will tell you about his friend who runs a museum. He will also give you the Critterpedia app

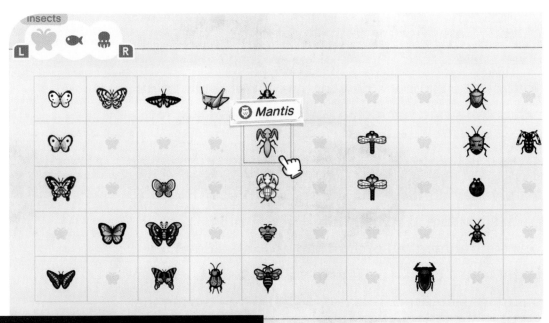

 Display Pictures Close Ⓐ ⌐

The Critterpedia app logs which wildlife you have captured so far. You can also read interesting facts about the creatures you have caught by clicking on them.

for your NookPhone so you can keep track of which wildlife **species** you've caught so far. Soon, an owl named Blathers will come to town to start a museum on your island. Once he arrives and gets set up, you'll be able to donate wildlife and fossils to fill the museum's exhibits. Filling up your museum is one of the most fun parts of the game, so always be on the lookout for new things to give Blathers.

You might find yourself wondering how to reach certain parts of your island. For example, a river might block you from reaching land on the other side. Or a cliff might prevent you from climbing up to a higher level. Keep working with Tom Nook and Blathers and you will soon acquire a couple of useful tools: a pole and a ladder. The pole will let you vault across rivers, while the ladder lets you reach higher areas. Later on, you'll be able to build bridges, ramps, and stairs. But for now, these tools will be essential for getting around.

One of the other things you'll want to focus on is befriending your fellow island settlers. There are hundreds of possible villager characters in *Animal Crossing: New Horizons.* While the two you start out with are random, more will continue to move to your town one by one until they reach a total of 10. (That doesn't count characters like Tom Nook and Blathers, who become a permanent part of everyone's islands.) Sometimes they will move in after visiting your island to camp for a day. Other times, you might come across characters when you visit other islands and invite them to your island.

Each villager has a different personality. You can make friends with them by talking to them often and giving them gifts. In exchange, they will sometimes give you gifts as well. On the other hand, you can

Cashmere

Oh my, now here's a face I haven't seen in quite some time! What on earth kept you away for so long?

Your fellow villagers will remember how you treat them and keep track of your actions.

Visiting Friends

Part of the fun of *Animal Crossing* is sharing your creations and seeing what your friends are doing in the game. You can do this by inviting friends to visit your village, or asking them if you can visit theirs. To do this, one player needs to visit the airport and talk to Orville, the bird behind the counter. Tell him you want visitors. You can either invite people from your Nintendo Switch friends list or ask for a Dodo Code. This means you can only play with people you actually know. No strangers can visit your island if you don't invite them.

Invite people from your friends list or share a Dodo Code with the friends you want to visit you. Then they can go to the airport on their own islands and fly to yours! Up to eight players at a time can be on the same island. That means you can play with seven of your friends at once. You can trade items, talk to each other's villagers, or just hang out!

ignore villagers if you don't like them. If you go long enough without talking to them, they might decide they want to move away. If you let them move, a different villager can move in to take their place.

If you play frequently, your island should be pretty full after a couple of weeks. There will be shops to visit, and tents will be replaced with permanent buildings. You'll have plenty of neighbors and all the tools you need to take care of the island. But even after all that work, there's still a lot more to do in *Animal Crossing*!

Chapter 4

Always Growing, Always Changing

One of the best things about *Animal Crossing* is that the fun never really ends. There is always something new to do. As time moves in real life, seasons will change in the game. You'll see different weather and hear different seasonal music. You'll even get to join in on special seasonal activities, such

I caught a koi!
I don't know why it's so shy...
or such a bad speller...

Some fish and bugs can only be caught at certain times of the year.

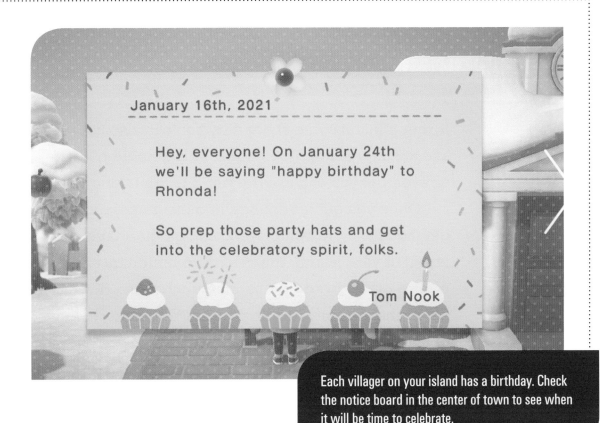

January 16th, 2021

Hey, everyone! On January 24th we'll be saying "happy birthday" to Rhonda!

So prep those party hats and get into the celebratory spirit, folks.

Tom Nook

Each villager on your island has a birthday. Check the notice board in the center of town to see when it will be time to celebrate.

as fishing contests and Halloween trick-or-treating. Check the notice board in the island plaza every time you play to see when different events are coming up.

Want to decorate your island? Just like in your house, you can drop furniture and other items anywhere you like and drag them around. Because it's the outdoors, you can also plant flowers, trees, and bushes. Simply dig a hole and drop in seeds or a seedling. Then fill the hole back in with dirt. Be sure to water your plants regularly until they bloom. Don't like where a plant is growing? Use a shovel to uproot it, then plant it somewhere else. You can also use your axe to simply chop trees down. This gets rid of them forever, but you can use the wood to craft things.

Once you get far enough into the game, you'll get the chance to completely change the shape and layout of your island. You can move buildings and bodies of water, add paths, and much more. However these changes are very expensive. You'll need plenty of Bells if you want to completely reshape your island. But if you keep at it, you're sure to get there eventually.

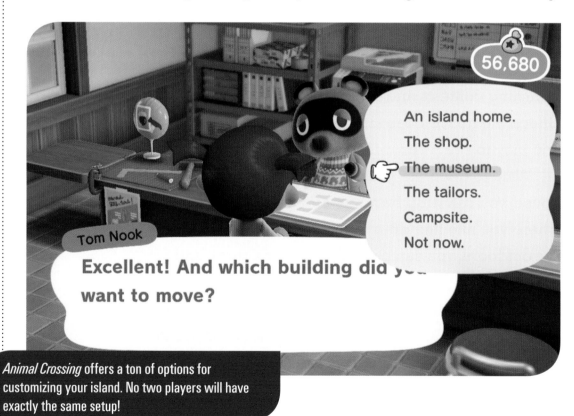

Animal Crossing offers a ton of options for customizing your island. No two players will have exactly the same setup!

Playing the Stalk Market

Want to make a lot of Bells as quickly as possible? Try buying and selling turnips. Every Sunday morning, a character named Daisy Mae will visit your island. You can purchase turnips from her. The price she sells them for changes each week. Throughout the week, you can sell the turnips back to Timmy and Tommy. The price they will pay changes twice a day. Sometimes it will be less than you paid Daisy Mae. Other times, it will be much more. If you can buy turnips at a low price and sell them at a high price, you'll make a lot of Bells. But there is also a risk you'll lose everything. The turnips go bad one week after you buy them. If you don't sell them before that, they become worthless!

Of course, you can always find ways to make your own fun in *Animal Crossing*. It's a game about creativity and relaxation, so feel free to experiment! If you need some ideas, try looking online to see what other players have done. You might be surprised at what you can do when you have a whole island to yourself!

Glossary

craft (KRAFT) make or build something

currency (KUR-uhn-see) a system of money

durable (DUR-uh-buhl) tough and long-lasting

fossils (FAH-suhlz) the preserved remains of living things from the distant past

hemisphere (HEM-uh-sfeer) half of the planet

inventory (IN-vuhn-toh-ree) a list of the items your character is carrying

plaza (PLAH-zuh) a public space often located in the central area of a town

species (SPEE-sheez) a particular category of animals or other living things

tanukis (ta-NOO-kees) animals that look similar to raccoons, but are more closely related to foxes

virtual (VUR-choo-uhl) existing in a computer program, but not in real life

Find Out More

BOOKS

Cunningham, Kevin. *Video Game Designer*. Ann Arbor, MI: Cherry Lake Publishing, 2016.

Loh-Hagan, Virginia. *Video Games*. Ann Arbor, MI: Cherry Lake Publishing, 2021.

Powell, Marie. *Asking Questions About Video Games*. Ann Arbor, MI: Cherry Lake Publishing, 2016.

WEBSITES

Animal Crossing Wiki
https://animalcrossing.fandom.com/wiki/Animal_Crossing:_New_Horizons
This fan-created site is packed with info about every detail of the *Animal Crossing* games.

Island News — *Animal Crossing: New Horizons*
https://www.animal-crossing.com/new-horizons/news
Keep up to date with the latest official news updates about *Animal Crossing*.

Index

About the Author

Josh Gregory is the author of more than 150 books for kids. He has written about everything from animals to technology to history. A graduate of the University of Missouri–Columbia, he currently lives in Chicago, Illinois.